SURVIVAL ZONE

SURVIVE A BLIZZARD

BY CHRIS BOWMAN

TORQUE™

BELLWETHER MEDIA · MINNEAPOLIS, MN

Are you ready to take it to the extreme? Torque books thrust you into the action-packed world of sports, vehicles, mystery, and adventure. These books may include dirt, smoke, fire, and chilling tales. **WARNING** : read at your own risk.

This edition first published in 2017 by Bellwether Media, Inc.

No part of this publication may be reproduced in whole or in part without written permission of the publisher. For information regarding permission, write to Bellwether Media, Inc., Attention: Permissions Department, 5357 Penn Avenue South, Minneapolis, MN 55419.

Library of Congress Cataloging-in-Publication Data

Names: Bowman, Chris, 1990- author.
Title: Survive a Blizzard / by Chris Bowman.
Description: Minneapolis, MN : Bellwether Media, Inc., [2017] | Series:
  Torque: Survival Zone | Includes bibliographical references and index. |
  Audience: 007-012. | Audience: Grades 3 through 7.
Identifiers: LCCN 2015051374 | ISBN 9781626174412 (hardcover : alk.
  paper)
Subjects: LCSH: Blizzards–Juvenile literature. | Severe storms–Juvenile
  literature.
Classification: LCC QC926.37 .B68 2017 | DDC 613.6/9–dc23
LC record available at https://lccn.loc.gov/2015051374

Printed in the United States of America, North Mankato, MN.

TABLE OF CONTENTS

A LONG + RIDE

February 19, 2012 is a snowy morning near Craig, Colorado. Teenagers Justin McAlexander and Jesse and Mason Burke are going snowmobiling in the mountains. They gather supplies and set off.

Soon, they encounter deep powder. Their snowmobiles begin to sink! The boys dig out their sleds, but they keep getting stuck. Justin calls for help on a cell phone. They are **stranded** for the night.

"I knew we were going to stay out there so I might as well make the best of it and get ready."
-Jesse Burke

"Dig a pit, collect more firewood, and keep the fire going. And wait, don't move, stay put."
-Justin McAlexander

They dig a pit and cover it with a blanket for shelter. Mason collects dry wood for a fire. Soon, a blizzard forms.

They spend the night trying to stay warm. When they run out of wood, they use fuel from a snowmobile. Rescuers find them in the morning. One boy has **frostbite** on his foot. But they survived the blizzard!

WILD WINTER STORMS

Blizzards are strong winter storms that last at least three hours. They always have high winds, blowing snow, and low **visibility**. Some blizzards do not make new snow!

Meteorologists track winter storms with **satellites** and **radar**. They send out warnings when blizzards form. Still, blizzards can grow quickly. It is important to always be prepared.

HOW A BLIZZARD FORMS

Strong blizzard winds form when warm and cold air meet. The warm air rises up. Cold air rushes in to fill the space, creating wind. If the temperature is around 32 degrees Fahrenheit (0 degrees Celsius), moisture in the air will fall as snow.

cold air

warm air

HIGH SPEEDS

To be considered a blizzard, the wind speed must be at least 35 miles (56 kilometers) per hour!

CAUGHT OUTSIDE

Shelter is your first concern during a blizzard. If there are buildings in sight, go to one quickly. But if you cannot see any shelters, it is safer to stay where you are.

Blowing snow can cause **whiteouts**. It is easy to get lost in these conditions. Staying put can help rescuers find you more quickly.

BLIZZARD SAFETY STEPS

1. Find shelter

2. Cover skin with dry clothes

3. Build a fire

STRINGS ATTACHED

If you need to leave a building, tie a rope to yourself and the building. Then you can easily find your way back.

Getting out of the wind is important. **Windchill** makes temperatures feel colder. Look for a nearby natural shelter such as a cave.

If one is not around, you can build a shelter. Piling snow makes a windbreak. You could also dig a **trench** and cover it with a blanket. If trees and branches are around, you can build a lean-to.

TYPES OF SHELTERS

snow cave

lean-to

windbreak

trench

In some areas, making a snow cave might be easiest. Find an area of deep snow. Dig out a hole big enough to crawl into.

As you get deeper, make the tunnel taller and wider. Poke a small hole in the top for **ventilation**. Then cover the entrance to trap in heat.

TRAP DOOR

Use something other than snow for the door. Snow can melt and form a layer of ice. This might trap you in the cave.

Staying warm and dry is important in a blizzard. Cover all skin and put on any extra clothing to protect from frostbite and **hypothermia**.

WINTER SURVIVAL KIT

For winter journeys on foot, be sure to have the following items:

extra batteries | warm boots | first aid kit | flashlight | food | layered clothing

matches | small shovel | water bottle | cell phone | extra clothing

If you can, build a fire to provide heat and dry wet clothes. Fire can also melt snow for drinking. After the storm, build a big fire or lay bright clothes on the snow. These signal to rescuers.

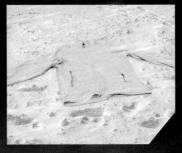

COLD AS ICE

Eating snow lowers your body temperature. Melt it first and then drink it.

IN THE CAR

Sometimes people get trapped in cars during blizzards. If this happens, stay in the car. Tie a bright piece of cloth to the antenna to help people find you.

STAY ACTIVE

Move around inside the car often to stay warm. Activities like sit-ups and push-ups help keep your body temperature normal.

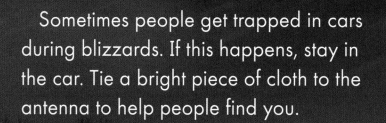

Run the engine for ten minutes each hour. Crack the windows for fresh air, and clear any snow around the tailpipe. **Fumes** from the **exhaust** can be deadly.

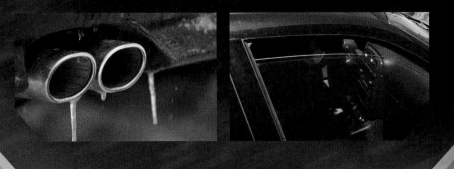

WINTER CAR KITS

Blizzard kits for the car should include everything for going outside, as well as:

 blankets

 sand or salt

 tool kit

 road maps

 bottled water

 flares

 emergency radio

 phone charger

hat

 gloves

STAYING ✚ INDOORS

The safest place to be during a blizzard is inside. But sometimes storms knock out heat and power. Buildings can become cold quickly.

Stay in one room to keep warm. Seal off other rooms with towels under the doors. Covering windows at night also keeps heat in. Stock up on food and drinks. Bundle up and stay relaxed!

FIRE IT UP

If possible, stay in a room with a fireplace. Only build a fire inside if there is a place for it.

exhaust—waste gases from a car's engine

frostbite—a condition in which skin and tissue are damaged because of cold temperatures

fumes—gas that smells strongly and is dangerous to breathe

hypothermia—a condition in which the body loses heat faster than it can produce it; hypothermia causes body systems to shut down.

meteorologists—scientists who study and predict the weather

radar—a device that sends out radio waves and maps their reflections; radar helps meteorologists predict the weather.

satellites—machines in space that move around Earth to help meteorologists predict the weather

stranded—left in a place with no way to get out

trench—a long hole dug into the snow

ventilation—a way to allow fresh air into a closed space

visibility—the ability to see

whiteouts—blizzards in which blowing snow makes it nearly impossible to see

windchill—the effect in which wind makes the air feel colder than it really is

AT THE LIBRARY

Kostigen, Thomas. *Extreme Weather: Surviving Tornadoes, Sandstorms, Hailstorms, Blizzards, Hurricanes, and More!* Washington, D.C.: National Geographic, 2014.

Markovics, Joyce L. *Blitzed by a Blizzard.* New York, N.Y.: Bearport Pub., 2010.

Tarshis, Lauren. *I Survived True Stories: Five Epic Disasters.* New York, N.Y.: Scholastic Inc., 2014.

ON THE WEB

Learning more about surviving a blizzard is as easy as 1, 2, 3.

1. Go to www.factsurfer.com.

2. Enter "survive a blizzard" into the search box.

3. Click the "Surf" button and you will see a list of related web sites.

With factsurfer.com, finding more information is just a click away.

INDEX